D0774073

ENGLISH with
CROSSWORDS

EUROPEAN LANGUAGE INSTITUTE

© ELI - European Language Institute s.r.l.
P.O. Box 6 - Recanati - Italy
Printed in Italy
By Tecnostampa s.r.l. - Loreto

Language teachers everywhere agree that learning vocabulary is greatly facilitated by the use of **visual** material. An illustrated word is learnt and retained more easily than one that is explained by using other words.

Our **crosswords** for beginners are consistent with this concept: they present the learner with an alternative to translation, and to the definition or description of a word through other words.

A team of language teaching experts has chosen **14 subjects**, and selected **20 words for each subject.** These are illustrated on the page that precedes each set of graded crosswords, which are arranged according to their theme.

On the first page there are ten numbered illustrations: using these, the young learner can insert the words into the right squares, so that the activity is also **an aid to spelling**.

On the second page, the remaining 10 illustrations are used the same way.

On page three, some words from pages one and two are used, and **on the fourth page**, the remaining illustrations from pages one and two are used in the same way.

At this stage the learner will have memorized the words and be able to insert them in the last crossword in the series.

By the time they have completed all the activities, young learners will be quite familiar with the vocabulary, thanks to the association of the word and illustration, and to the consolidation afforded by the repetitive nature of the activity.

This fun book is ideal for playing at home, especially during the holidays. **It's simple and it's fun, and it's a great help in learning vocabulary!**

La pratique moderne de l'enseignement des langues accorde de plus en plus d'importance à la **visualisation** car on est convaincu qu'un vocabulaire illustré peut être mémorisé plus vite qu'un mot expliqué simplement par d'autres mots.

L'emploi des «**mots croisés**» répond à cet objectif. Pour un premier niveau de connaissance de la langue, cet exercice est une alternative à la traduction, à la définition et à la description des mots. Des experts en didactique linguistique ont choisi **14 thèmes** et ont sélectionné d'une manière arbitraire **20 mots pour chacun des thèmes, illustrés** sur la page qui précède chaque série progressive de jeux.

La première page de jeux présente dix illustrations. L'élève peut placer les mots en s'aidant de l'illustration et en comptant le nombre de lettres.
Sur la deuxième page, il trouve les dix autres illustrations du thème.
Sur la troisième page, sont utilisées cinq illustrations de la première page et cinq de la deuxième page.
Sur la quatrieme, les cinq qui restent de la première page et les cinq qui restent de la deuxième page.
A ce point, l'élève est capable de se rappeler tous les mots et de les placer facilement **dans la dernière grille de la série.**
En complétant successivement les différents schémas, les élèves se familiarisent avec les mots et augmentent leur vocabulaire car l'image associée au mot et la répétitivité du jeu favorisent la mémorisation.
Ce livre de jeux peut être utilisé aussi par l'élève chez lui surtout pendant les vacances.

La pratica moderna dell'insegnament linguistico accorda sempre maggior importanza alla **visualizzazione**, nel la convinzione che un vocabolo illustrato s apprende in maniera più immediata e dure vole di una parola semplicemente spiega con altre parole.

L'uso delle **parole crociate** è coerente co questa idea.
Quest'attività ha lo scopo, ai primi livel di conoscenza della lingua, di trovare un'al ternativa alla traduzione, alla definizione alla descrizione delle parole. Un'equipe d esperti della didattica linguistica hanno sce to **quattordici temi** e selezionato in mod arbitrario **20 parole per ogni tema**, illustr te nella pagina che precede ciascuna seri tematica e graduata dei giochi.

La prima pagina di giochi contiene die ci illustrazioni. Il ragazzo con l'aiuto de l'immagine e contando il numero del lettere può inserire le parole nelle caselle a propriate.
L'attività, oltre ad essere un **esercizio di a prendimento** di nuovi vocaboli, è anche **ut le per l'ortografia**.
Nella seconda pagina, sono utilizzate an logamente le rimanenti dieci immagini de tema.
Nella terza pagina, sono utilizzate 5 im magini delle prima e 5 della seconda.
Nella quarta pagina, le rimanenti 5 dell prima e 5 della seconda.
A questo punto il ragazzo è in grado di r cordare tutte le parole e inserirle agevolmer te **nell'ultimo schema della serie.**
L'immagine associata al vocabolo e il ripe tersi del gioco favoriscono la memoriz zazione.
Il presente libro-gioco può essere utilizza to dagli studenti anche a casa, particola mente durante le vacanze.
Controllare le lettere di ogni parola stan pata e inserirla nelle caselle giuste: ecco u modo divertente per **arricchire il lessico**

Im modernen Fremdsprachenunterricht wird der **Visualisierung** eine immer größere Bedeutung beigemessen. Ein illustriertes Wort lernt man schneller und leichter als eines, das nur einfach erklärt oder im Wörterbuch herausgesucht wird. Außerdem bleibt es viel länger im Gedächtnis haften.

Kreuzworträtsel sind eine ideale Übungsform, um neue Vokabeln zu lernen und den Wortschatz «spielend» zu bereichern. Man kann so ein Wort ohne Übersetzung und ohne komplizierte Definitionen und Umschreibungen verstehen und direkt erlernen.

Eine auf Fremdsprachen-Didaktik spezialisierte Expertengruppe hat **vierzehn Themen** ausgesucht und für jedes Thema willkürlich **20 Wörter** gewählt, die auf der vor den Kreuzwortfeldern stehenden Seite illustriert dargestellt sind.

Die **erste** Seite zeigt die ersten 10 Wörter in Bildern. Der Lernende kann mit Hilfe der einzelnen Bilder und durch Abzählen der Buchstaben die Wörter in die richtigen Felder einsetzen. Diese unterhaltsame Übung ist sowohl zum Vokabellernen als auch für die Rechtschreibung sehr nützlich. Auf der **zweiten** Seite sieht man die anderen 10 Bilder des Themas.

Die **dritte** Seite zeigt 5 Bilder der ersten Seite und 5 Bilder der zweiten Seite. Auf der **vierten** Seite werden die übrigen 5 Bilder der ersten und die übrigen 5 Bilder der zweiten Seite abgebildet.

Nach diesen Einsetzübungen hat sich der Lernende diese neuen Wörter gut eingeprägt, und er kann sie nun ohne Schwierigkeiten in die Felder des letzten zur Thematik gehörenden Kreuzworträtsels einsetzen.

Dieses neue Spiel-Buch kann auch zu Hause verwendet werden und ist eine nette Freizeitbeschäftigung in den Ferien.

La moderna metodología lingüística concede cada vez mayor importancia a **la imagen**, ya que está demostrado que una palabra ilustrada se aprende de un modo más inmediato y duradero que una palabra explicada con otras palabras.

El uso de los **crucigramas** es coherente con este principio. Esta actividad se propone, en el ámbito de los niveles más elementales de conocimiento, encontrar una alternativa a la traducción, a la definición y descripción de las palabras. Un equipo de expertos en didáctica linguística ha elegido **14 temas** y ha seleccionado **20 palabras por tema**. Estas palabras van ilustradas en cuatro páginas siguiendo un orden temático y gradual en los juegos.

En la primera página de juegos, hay diez ilustraciones. El alumno, con la ayuda de la imagen y contando el número de letras, va colocando las palabras en su lugar correspondiente. Este ejercicio, además de **favorecer el aprendizaje** de nuevas palabras, es **útil para la ortografía**.

En la segunda página, se utilizan del mismo modo las otras diez ilustraciones del tema.

En la tercera página, se usan 5 imágines de la primera y 5 de la segunda.

En la cuarta página, las otras 5 de la primera y de la segunda.

Al final de este proceso el alumno ha memorizado todas las palabras y las puede colocar ágilmente **en el último esquema de la serie**.

Los alumnos, completando sucesivamente los distintos crucigramas, se familiarizan con las palabras, aumentan su vocabulario porque la imagen asociada a la palabra y la repetición del juego les facilitan su memorización. Los estudiantes pueden utilizar este libro-juego también en casa, sobre todo durante las vacaciones.

Controlar las letras de cada palabra y colocarlas en el espacio correspondiente: una manera divertida de enriquecer el léxico.

a rabbit

a bull

a horse

a cock

a donkey

a sheep

a dog

a cat

a cow

a mouse

a duck

a hen

a bird

a goose

a chick

a pig

a frog

a turkey

a butterfly

a goat

(1)

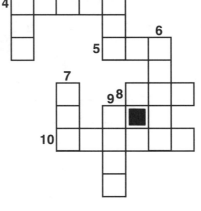
(2)

(3)

(4)

(5)

(6)

(7)

(8)

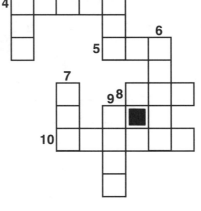
(9)

(10)

1

2

3

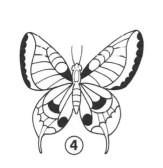

4

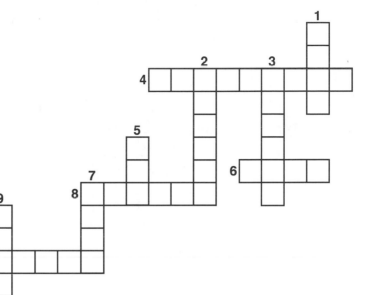

1

2   3

4

5

6

7

8

9

10

5

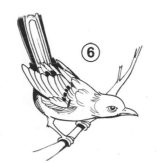

6

7

8

9

10

THE HOUSE

a ceiling

a wall

a chimney

a floor

a roof

a window

a door

a gate

a bedroom

a dining-room

a kitchen

a bathroom

a hall

steps

stairs

a block of flats

a house

a flat

a garage

a garden

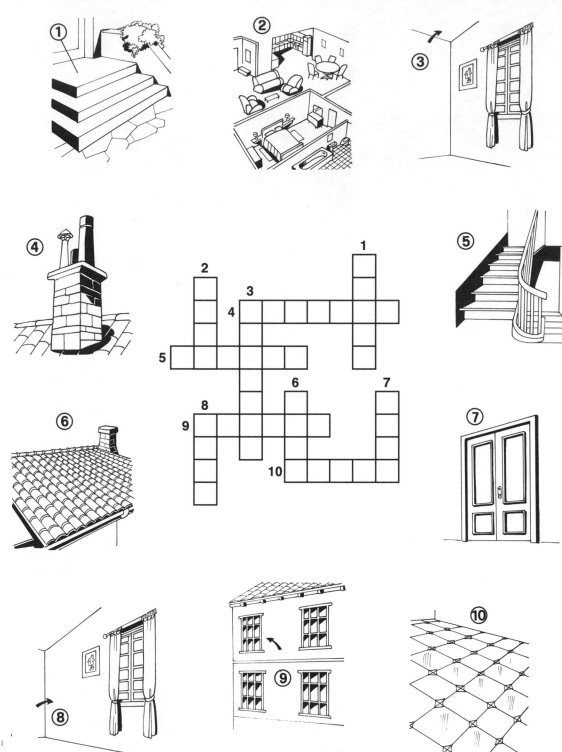

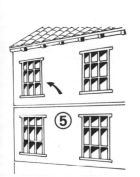

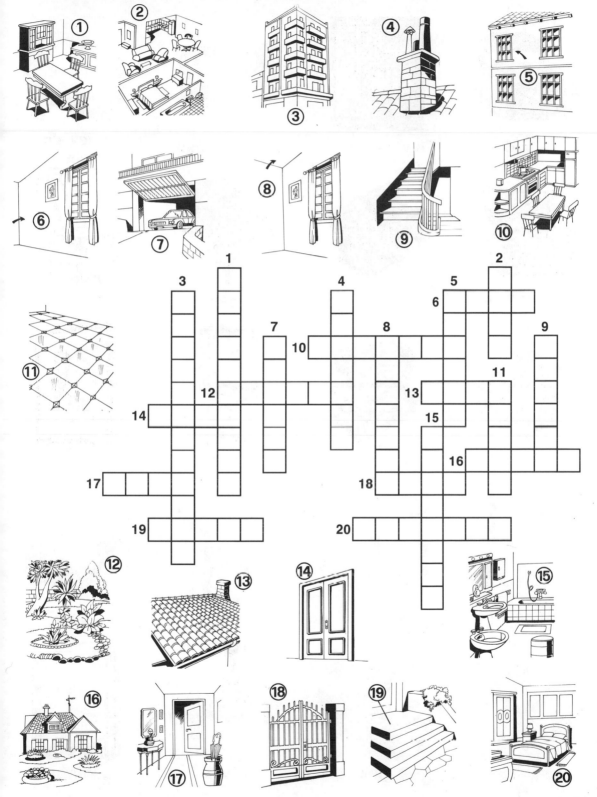

a bed

a wardrobe

an alarm-clock

a television set

an armchair

a sofa

a table

a chair

a cushion

drawers

a lamp

a picture

a refrigerator

a washing-machine

a washbasin

a bath

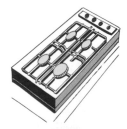

a cooker

a sink

a tap

a mirror

18

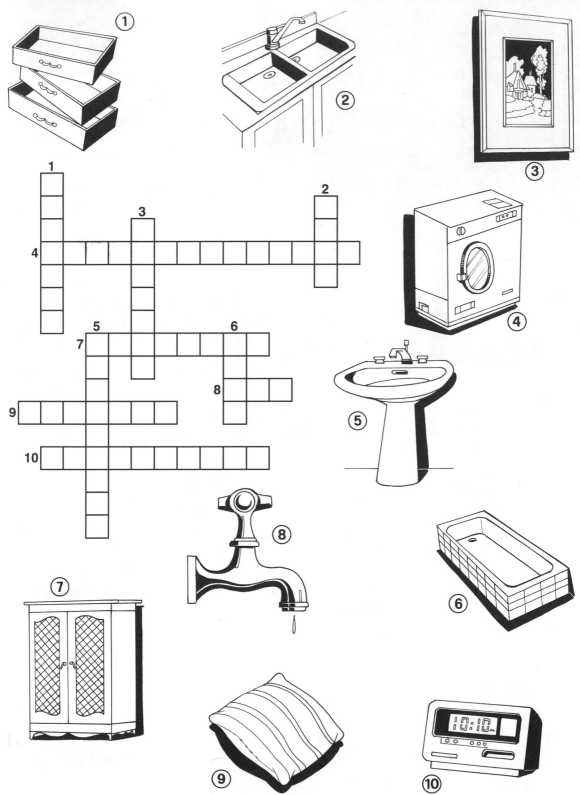

①

②

③

④

⑤

⑥

⑦

⑧

⑨

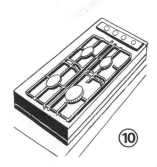

⑩

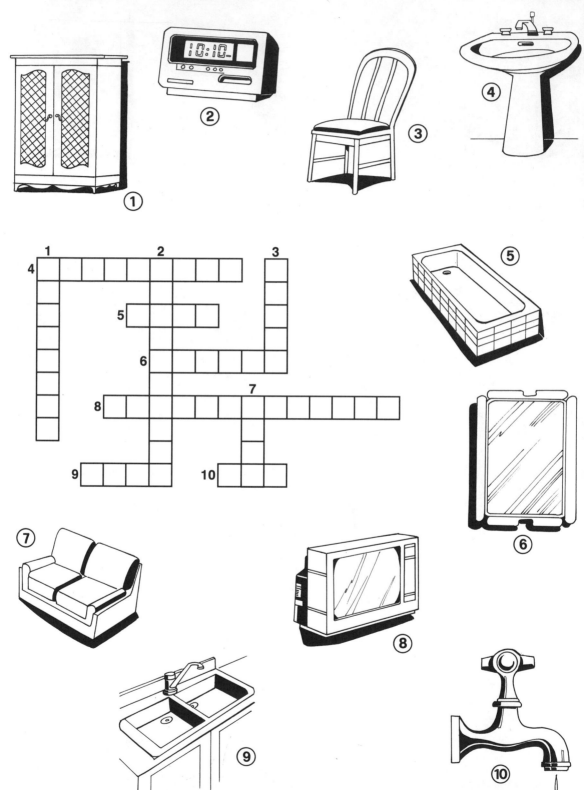

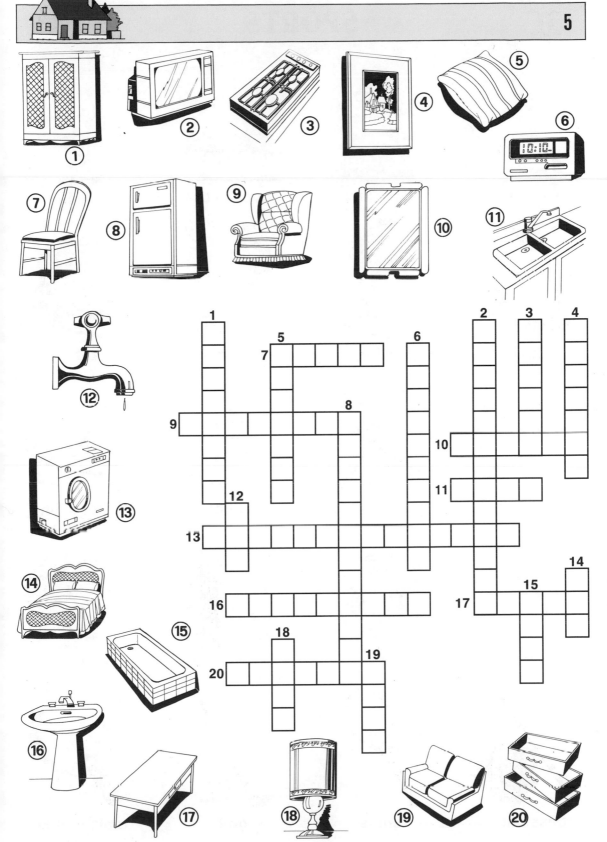

SPORTS

running

high-jump

gymnastics

judo

riding

cycling

fencing

skating

swimming

rowing

sailing

water-skiing

skiing

football

basketball

volley-ball

baseball

tennis

golf

table-tennis

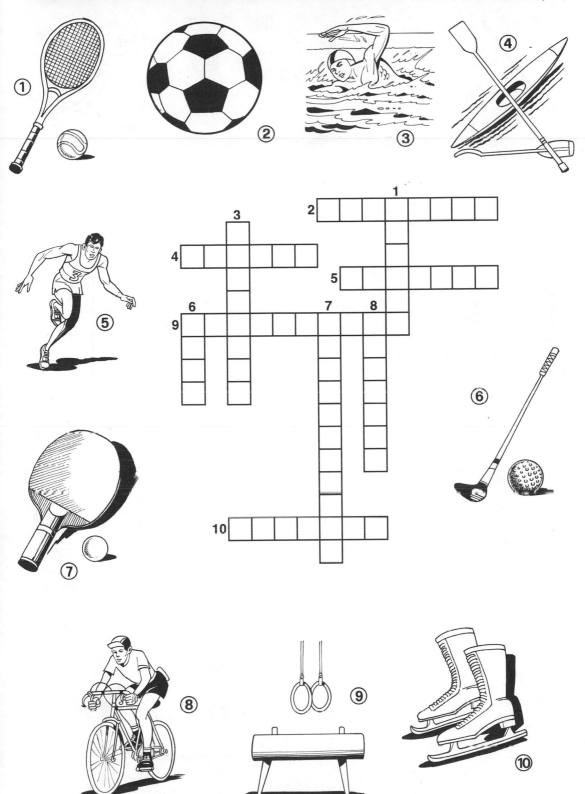

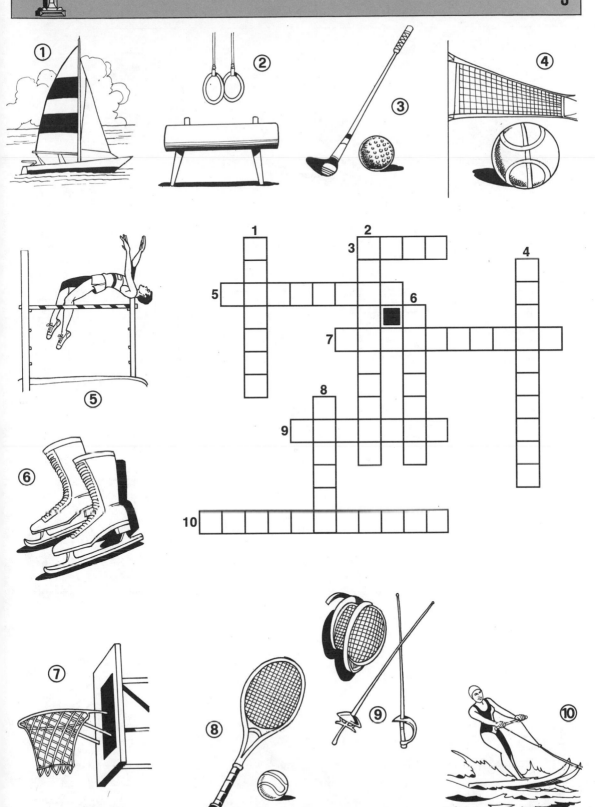

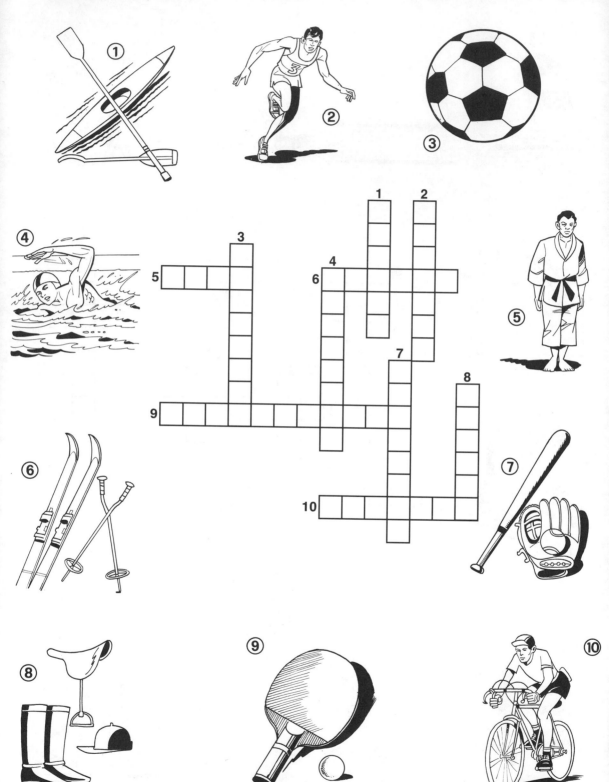

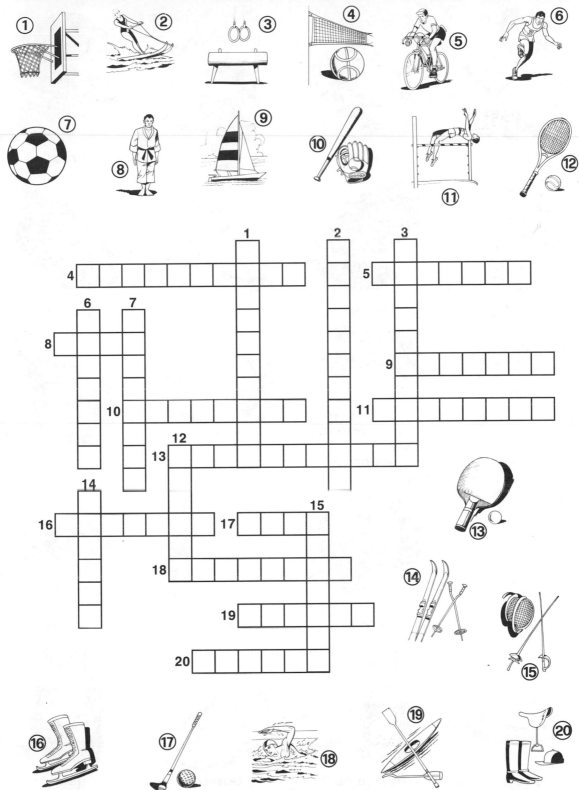

 # FOOD AND DRINK

coffee

tea

milk

bread

biscuits

meat

fish

chicken

cheese

sausages

eggs

ham

ice-cream

cake

water

sugar

soup

fruit juice

butter

jam

30

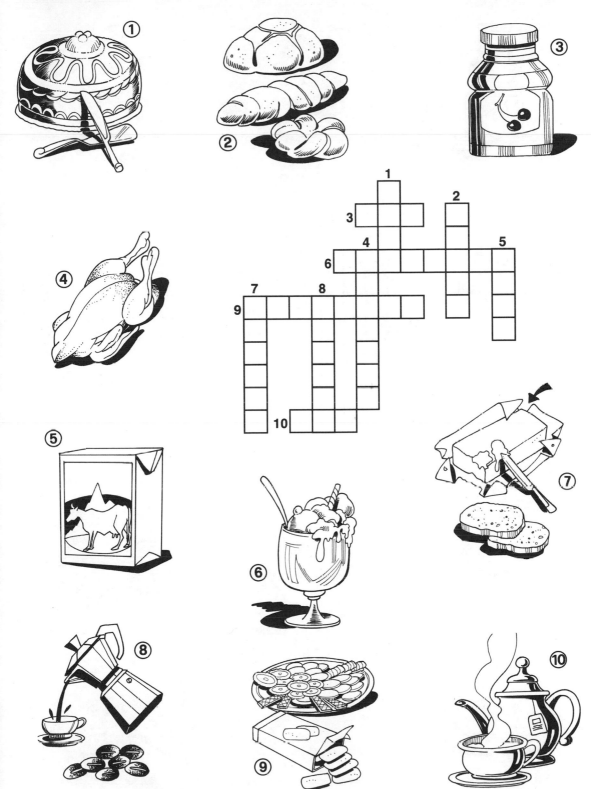

an apple

a pear

grapes

strawberries

peaches

an apricot

an orange

a lemon

a melon

a banana

a pineapple

plums

cherries

a cabbage

potatoes

tomatoes

a lettuce

carrots

peas

a mushroom

1

2

3

4

```
        1 □□□□□□□□
      2 □
        □
    3 □       4 □□□□□□ 5 □□□ 6 □
    7 □
    8 □□□□□      9 □□□□□
        □
        □      10 □□□□
```

5

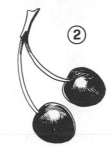
6

7

8

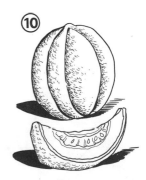
9

10

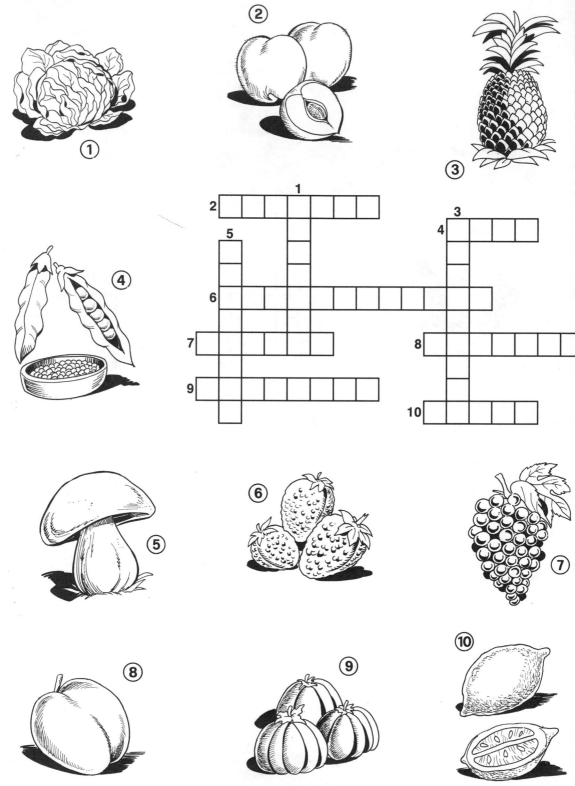

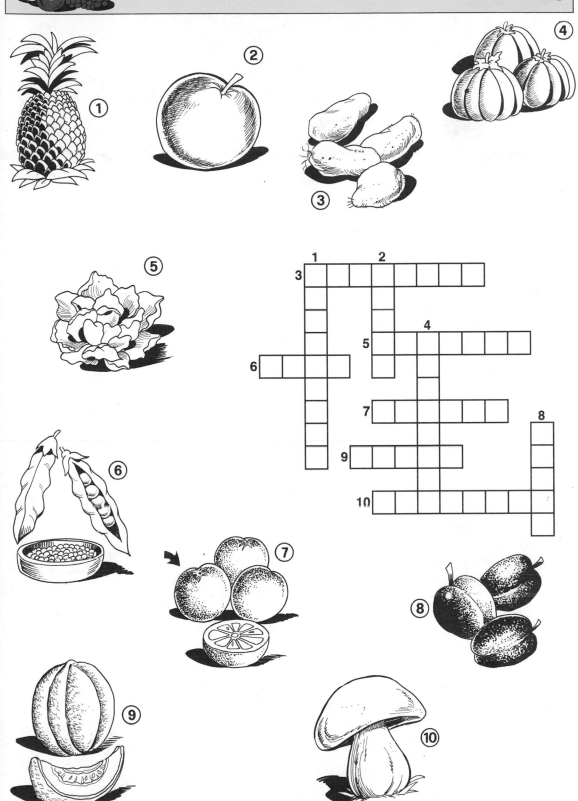

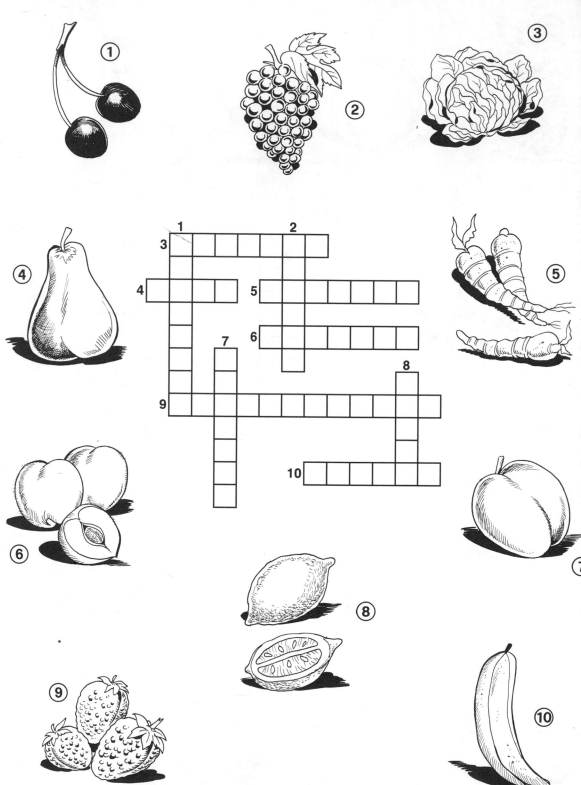

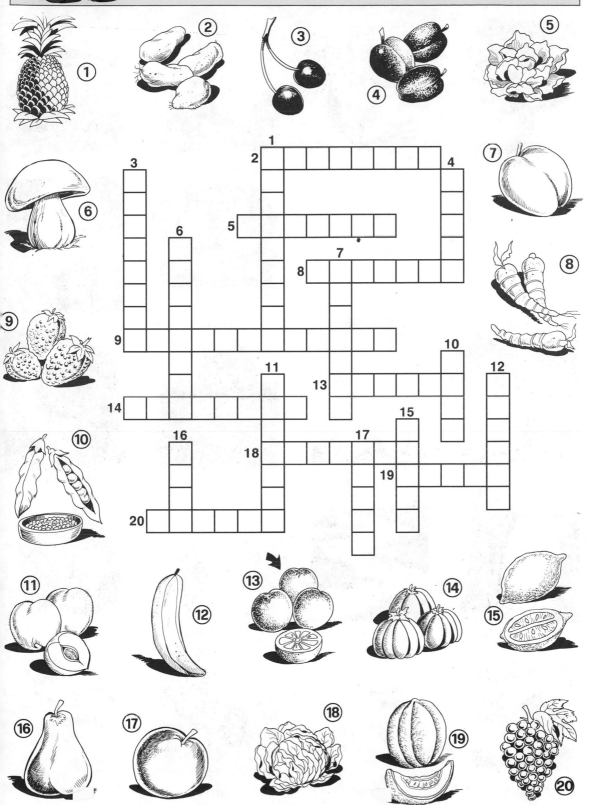

NATURE

 a tree

 a flower

 mountains

 a hill

 the sun

 clouds

 stars

 the moon

 a rainbow

 the sky

 a field

 a wood

 a waterfall

 a river

 the sea

 a lake

 an island

 snow

 rain

 wind

①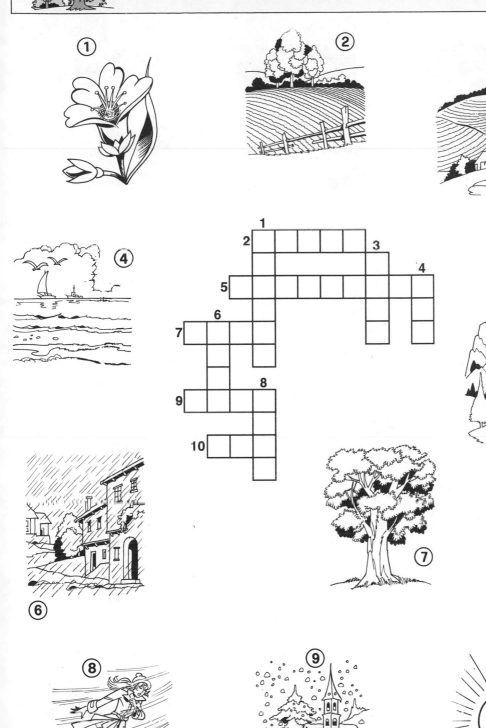

②

③

④

⑤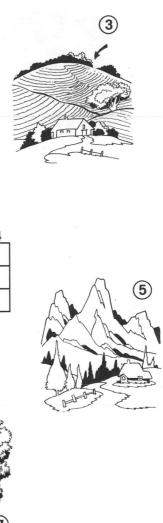

⑥

⑦

⑧

⑨

⑩

43

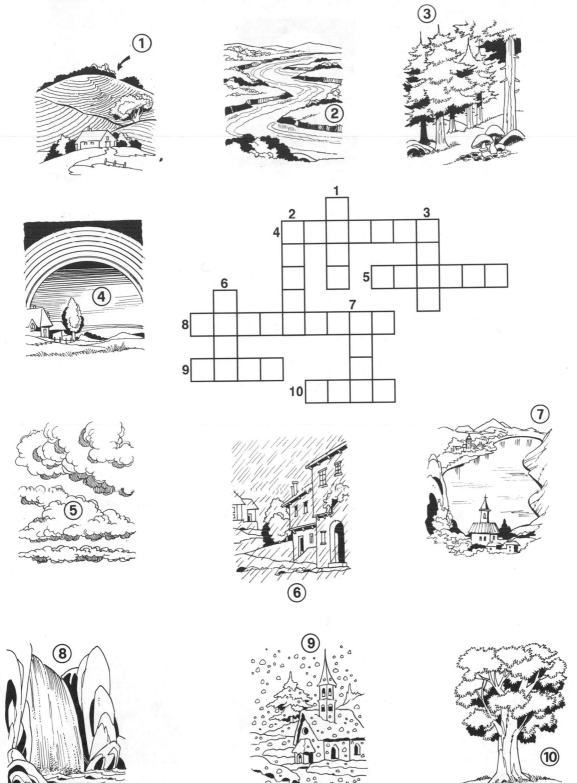

# IN TOWN

a school

a church

a hospital

a library

shops

a bank

a Post Office

a cinema

a hotel

a restaurant

a petrol-station

a factory

a stadium

a park

a square

a street

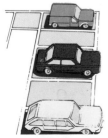
a parking-area

traffic-lights

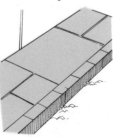
a pavement

a statue

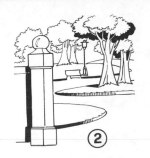

49

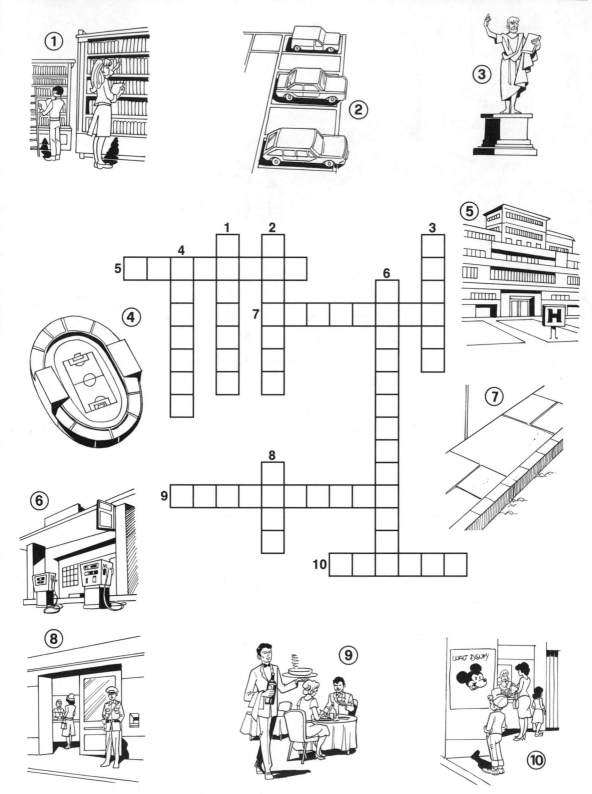

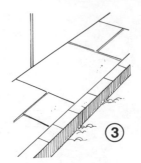

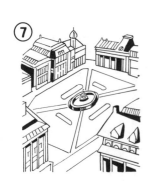

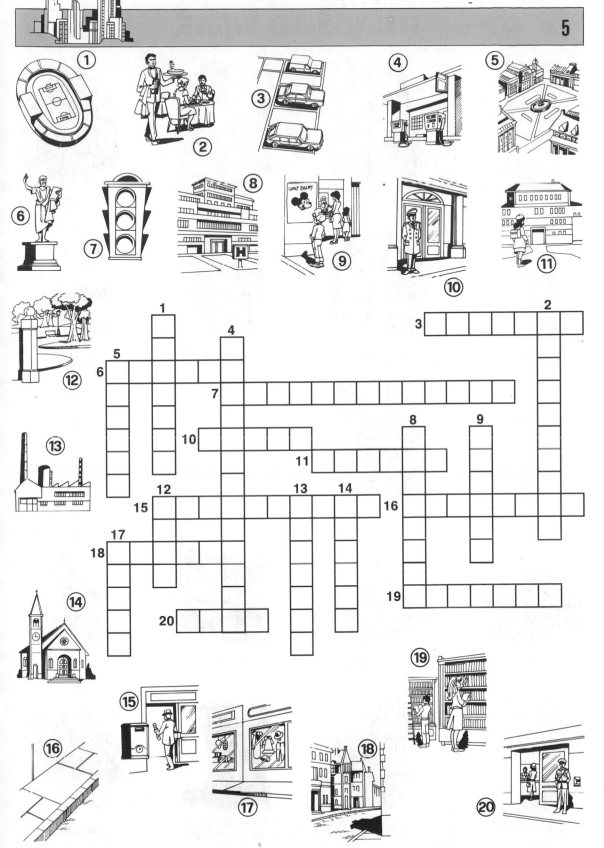

THINGS TO WEAR

a dress

a skirt

a shirt

a sweater

trousers

a jacket

a coat

a scarf

shorts

socks

underwear

a T-shirt

shoes

slippers

sandals

a tie

pyjamas

gloves

**wellingtons or
wellington boots**

a hat

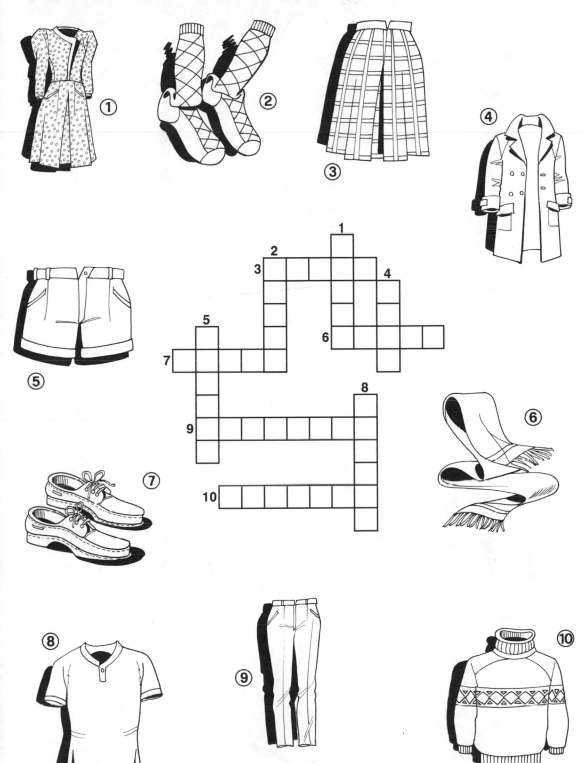

① ② ③ ④ ⑤ ⑥ ⑦ ⑧ ⑨ ⑩

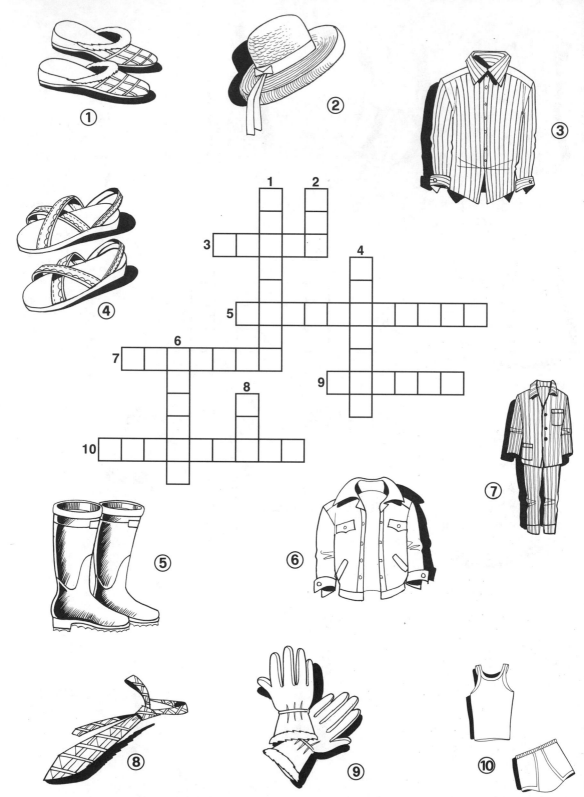

3

①

②

③

④

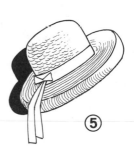

⑤

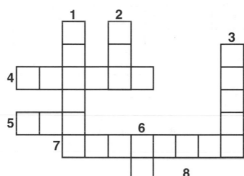

④ 4

⑤ 5

7

6

9 ⑧ 8

10

⑦

⑧

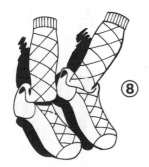

⑨

⑩

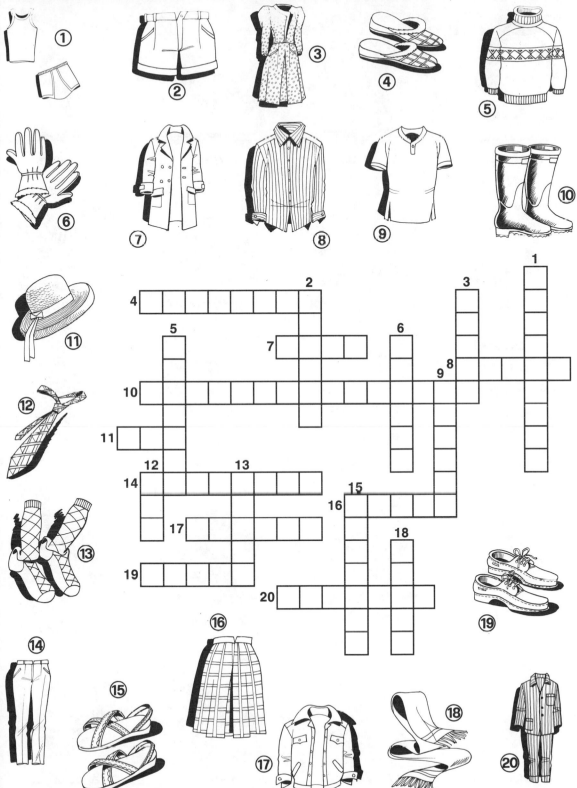

 a penguin

 a camel

 a deer

 a giraffe

 a panda

 a hippopotamus

 a tortoise

 a zebra

 a snake

 a rhinoceros

 a lion

 a tiger

 a kangaroo

 an elephant

 a gorilla

 a monkey

 a crocodile

 a wolf

 a seal

 a bear

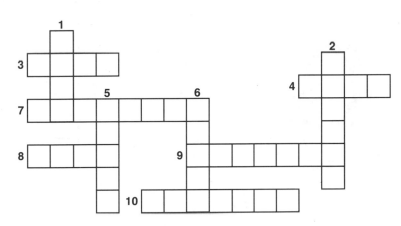

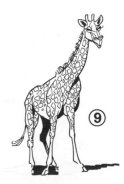

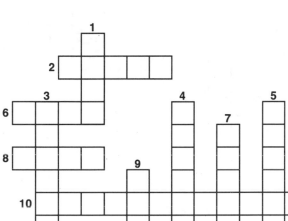

1

2

3

5

6

7

8

9

10

4

OPPOSITES

fast

slow

hot

cold

big

small

tall

short

long

short

fat

thin

good

bad

pretty

ugly

new

old

full

empty

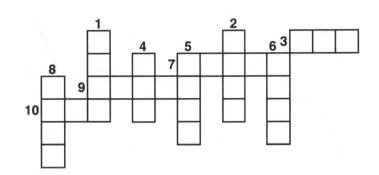

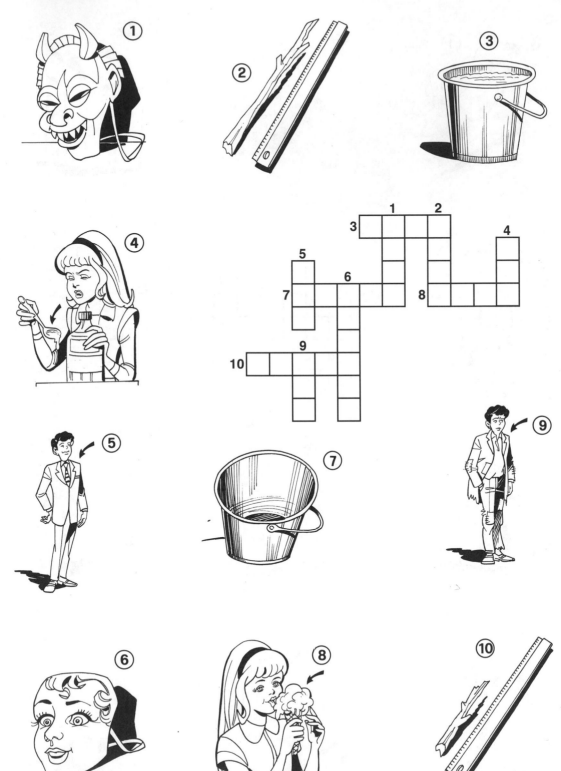

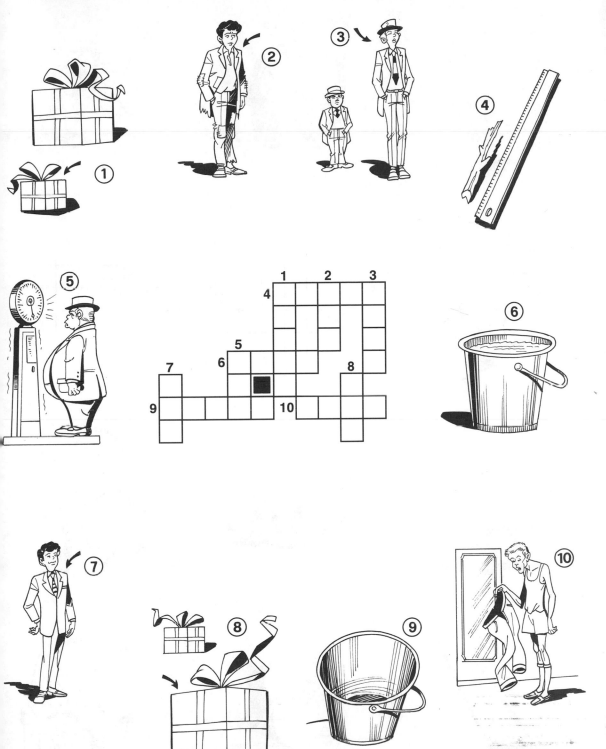

1

2

3

4

5

6

7

4

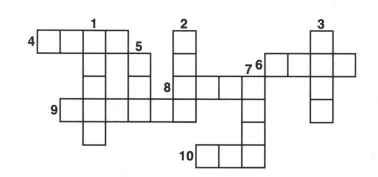

1   2   3

5   6   7

8

9

10

5

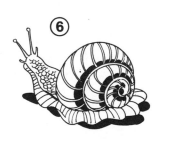

6

7

8

9

10

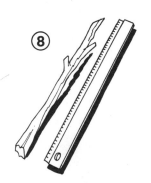

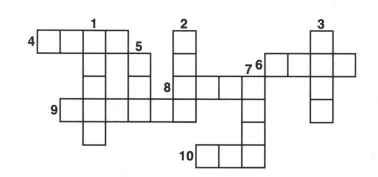

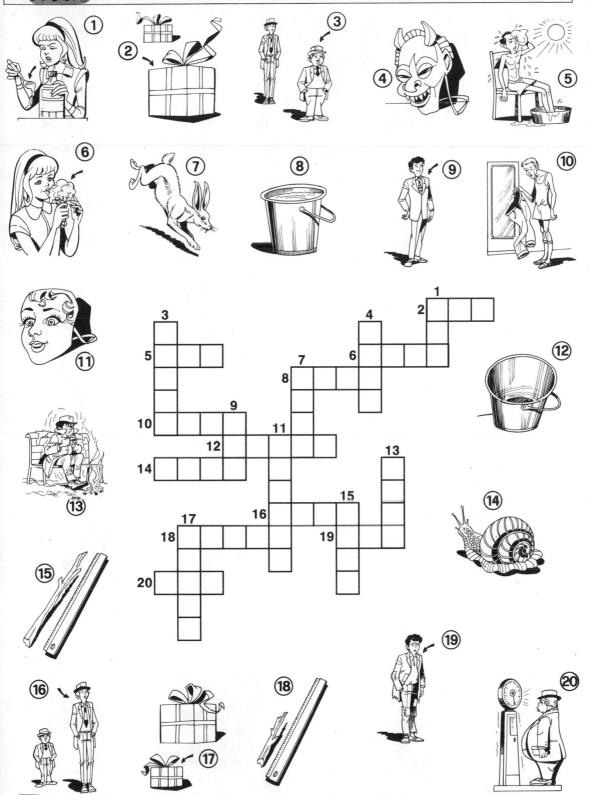

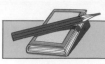

AT SCHOOL

a rubber

a pencil-case

an exercise-book

a pen

felt-pens

a pencil-sharpener

a book

paste

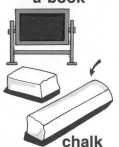

coloured pencils

scissors

chalk

a ruler

a blackboard

a stapler

a paint-brush

paints

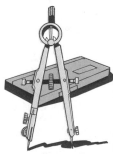

a pencil

a teacher

a waste-paper basket

a compass

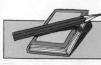

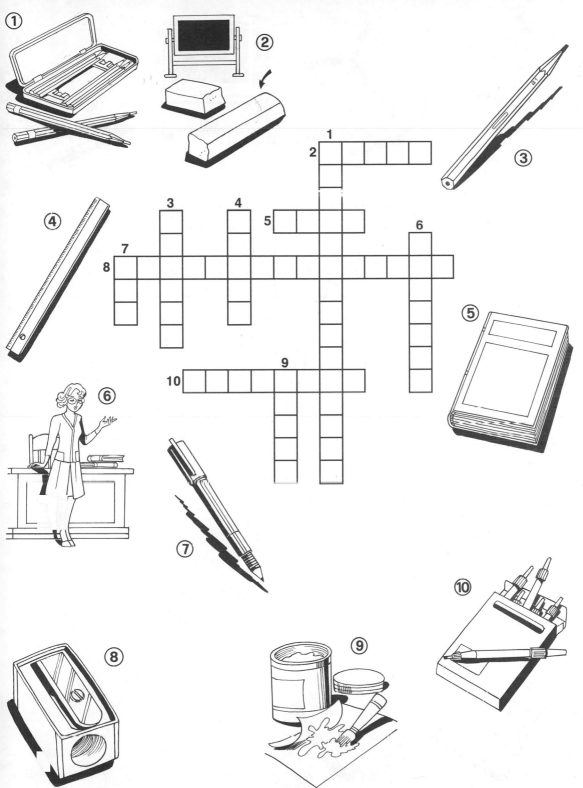

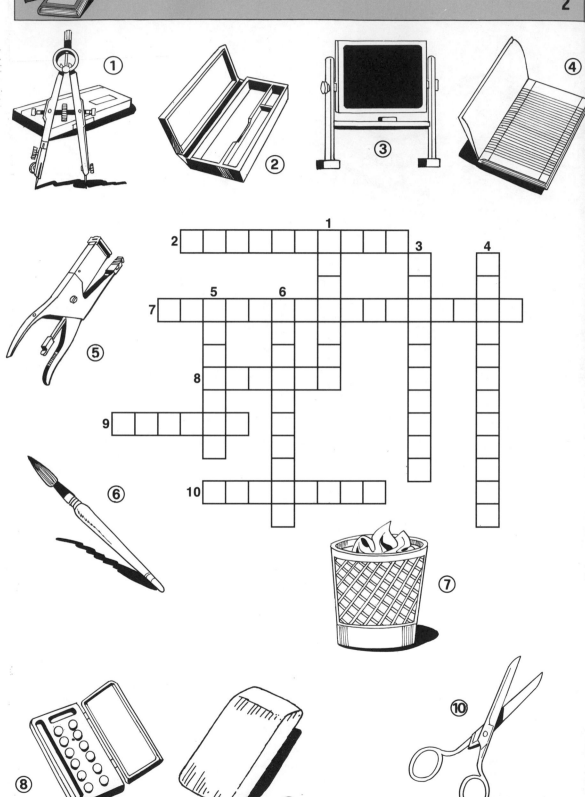

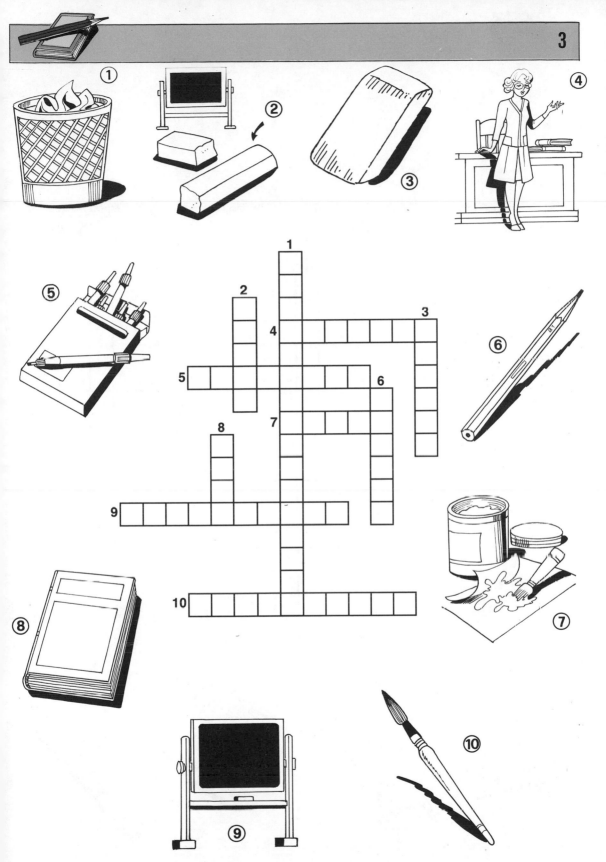

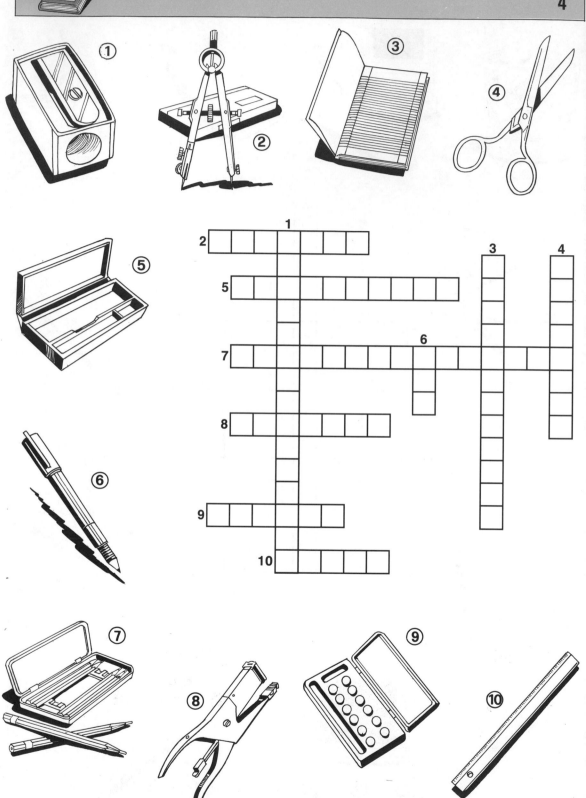

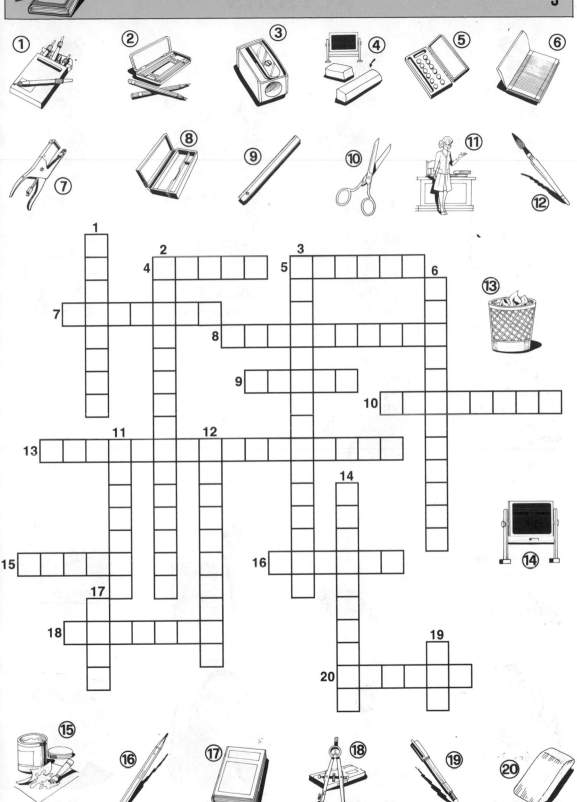

5

77

ACTIONS

to come down

to go up

to watch

to eat

to sleep

to go in

to come out

to drink

to write

to read

to fall

to pull

to push

to draw

to speak

to listen

to telephone

to walk

to cry

to laugh

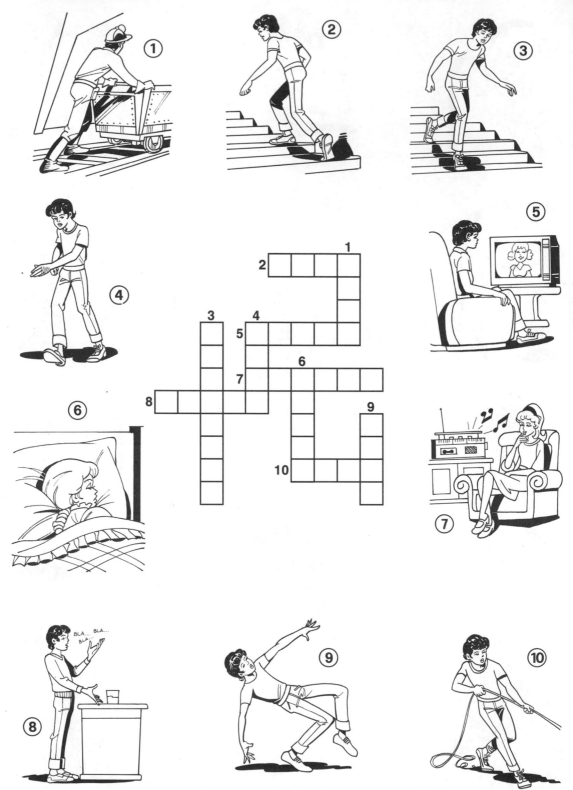

1

2

3

4

5

6

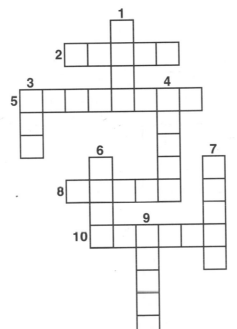

7

6

8

 # MEANS OF TRANSPORT

a bicycle

a moped

a motor-bike

a car

a van

a lorry

a tractor

a taxi

an ambulance

a fire-engine

a bus

an under-ground train

a train

a rowing-boat

a motor-boat

a ship

a helicopter

an aeroplane

a rocket

a space-ship

84

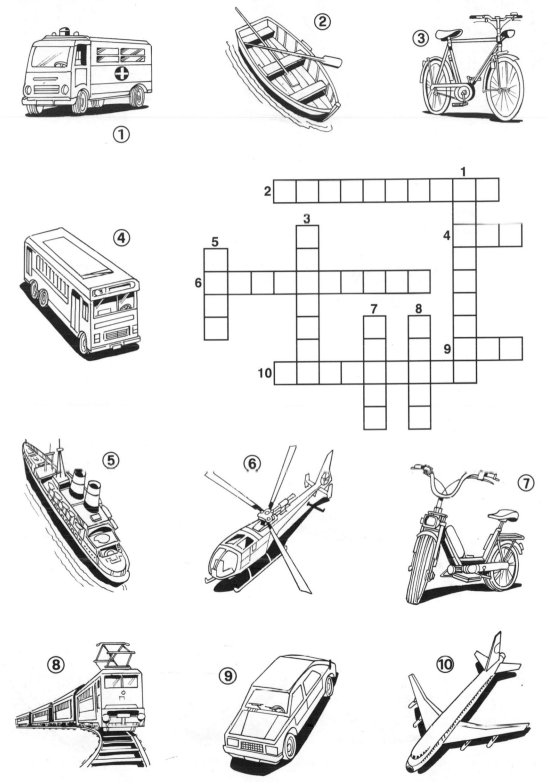

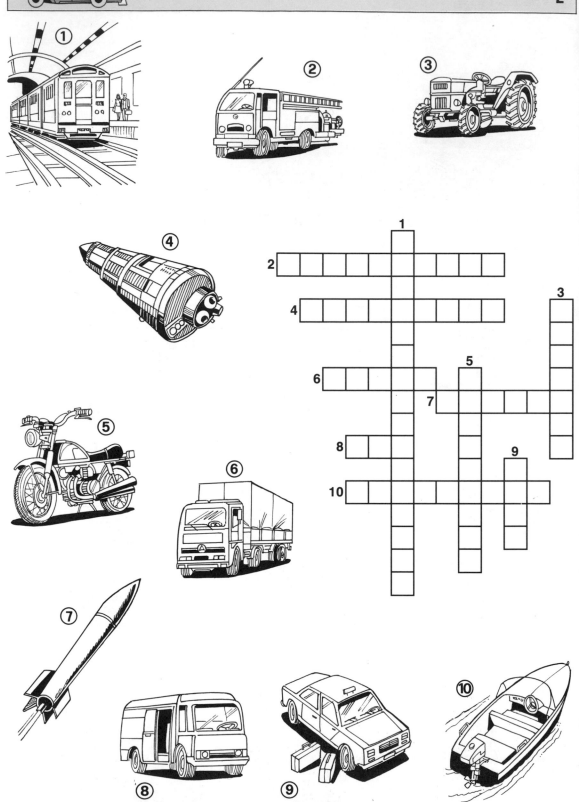

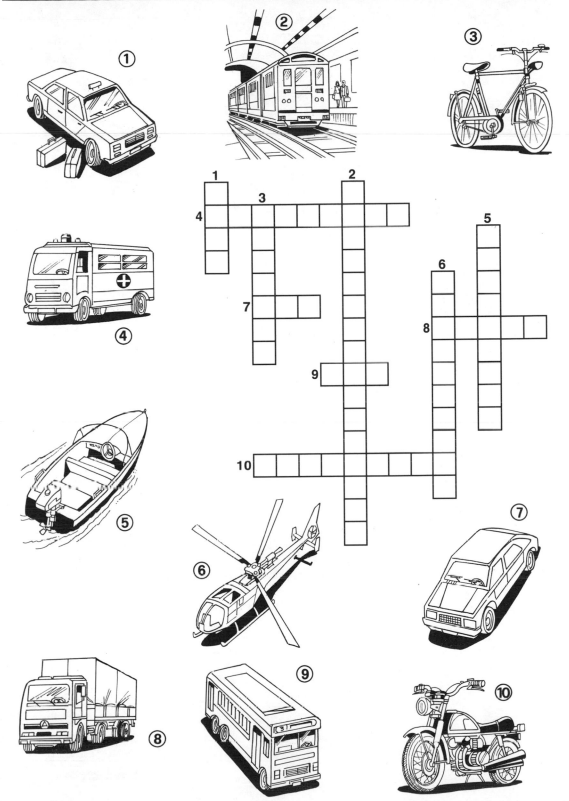

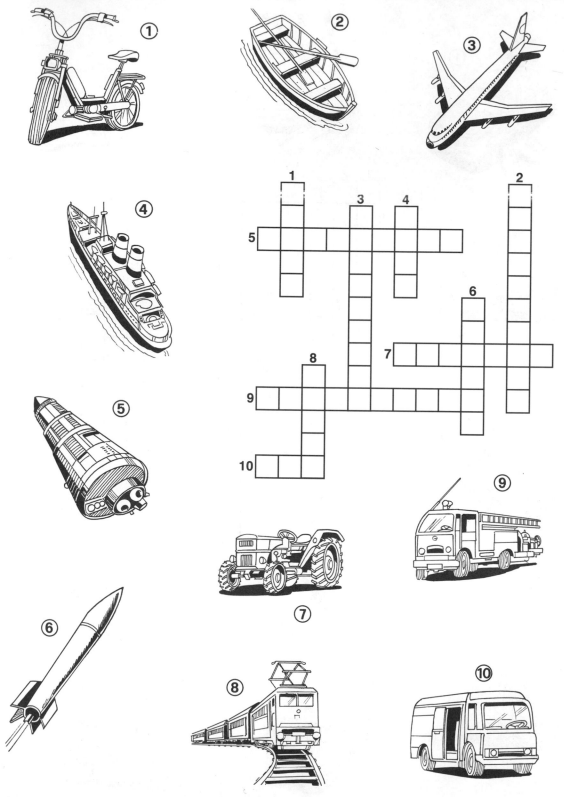

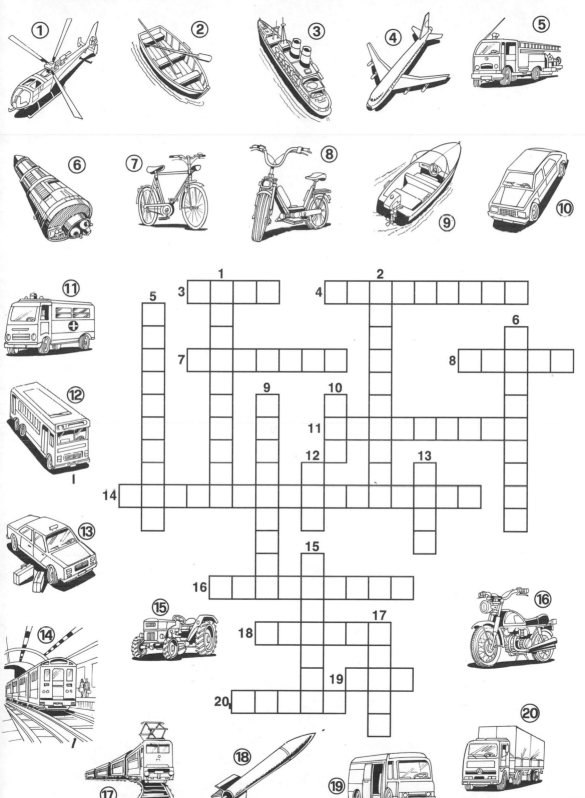

FARM ANIMALS

page 6

a bird	a cock	a frog	a mouse
a bull	a cow	a goat	a pig
a butterfly	a dog	a goose	a rabbit
a cat	a donkey	a hen	a sheep
a chick	a duck	a horse	a turkey

THE HOUSE

page 12

a bathroom	a dining-room	a garage	a roof
a block of flats	a door	a gate	stairs
a bedroom	a flat	a hall	steps
a ceiling	a floor	a house	a wall
a chimney	a garden	a kitchen	a window

FURNITURE AND FITTINGS

page 18

an alarm-clock	a cooker	a picture	a tap
an armchair	a cushion	a refrigerator	a television set
a bath	drawers	a sink	a wardrobe
a bed	a lamp	a sofa	a washbasin
a chair	a mirror	a table	a washing-machine

SPORTS

page 24

baseball	golf	rowing	swimming
basketball	gymnastics	running	table-tennis
cycling	high-jump	sailing	tennis
fencing	judo	skating	volley-ball
football	riding	skiing	water-skiing

FOOD AND DRINK

page 30

biscuits	chicken	ham	sausages
bread	coffee	ice-cream	soup
butter	eggs	jam	sugar
cake	fish	meat	tea
cheese	fruit juice	milk	water

FRUIT AND VEGETABLES

page 36

an apple	cherries	a mushroom	a pineapple
an apricot	grapes	an orange	plums
a banana	a lemon	peaches	potatoes
a cabbage	a lettuce	a pear	strawberries
carrots	a melon	peas	tomatoes

NATURE

page 42

clouds	a lake	a river	the sun
a field	the moon	the sea	a tree
a flower	mountains	the sky	a waterfall
a hill	rain	snow	wind
an island	a rainbow	stars	a wood

IN TOWN

page 48

a bank	a hospital	a petrol-station	a square
a car-park	a hotel	a Post Office	a stadium
a church	a library	a restaurant	a statue
a cinema	a park	a school	a street
a factory	a pavement	shops	a pavement

CLOTHES

page 54

a coat	pyjamas	shorts	a tie
a dress	sandals	a skirt	trousers
gloves	a scarf	slippers	a T-shirt
a hat	a shirt	socks	underwear
a jacket	shoes	a sweater	wellingtons

ON SAFARI

page 60

a bear	a giraffe	a monkey	a snake
a camel	a gorilla	a panda	a tiger
a crocodile	a hippopotamus	a penguin	a tortoise
a deer	a kangaroo	a rhinoceros	a zebra
an elephant	a lion	a seal	a wolf

OPPOSITES

page 66

bad	fast	new	slow
big	fat	old	small
cold	full	pretty	tall
good	hot	short	thin
empty	long	short	ugly

AT SCHOOL

page 72

a blackboard	an exercise book	a pen	a ruler
a book	felt-pens	a pencil	scissors
chalk	a paint-brush	a pencil-case	a stapler
coloured pencils	paints	a pencil-sharpener	a teacher
a compass	paste	a rubber	a waste-paper basket

ACTIONS

to come down	to eat	to listen	to speak
to come out	to fall	to pull	to telephone
to cry	to go in	to push	to walk
to draw	to go up	to read	to watch
to drink	to laugh	to sleep	to write

MEANS OF TRANSPORT

an aeroplane	a fire-engine	a motor-boat	a taxi
an ambulance	a helicopter	a rocket	a tractor
a bicycle	a lorry	a rowing-boat	a train
a bus	a moped	a ship	an underground train
a car	a motor-bike	a space-ship	a van

Printed in Italy by Tecnostampa